COMPETITIVE OBEDIENCE

A step-by-step guide

Paddy Coughlan

ABOUT THE AUTHOR

Paddy Coughlan joined his first Obedience dog club (Arden) 35 years ago. He was persuaded to take their instructors' course, and, after passing, has conducted classes ever since.

Paddy became a member of a branch of Birmingham and District Dog Training Club, eventually becoming branch chairman. He also became chairman of the newly-formed Hatchford Brook Dog Training Club in 1979, and remains so to date.

At this time, he acquired his first sheepdog, Sadghyl Meg, and began working her in competition. Meg won every class from pre-beginners to Championship Class 'C', taking Paddy to Crufts for the first time in 1978.

Paddy regularly judges, and has awarded Challenge Certificates in Obedience since 1985. He has served more than 20 years as one of the Midlands Area Representatives on the Obedience Liaison Council, and is currently in his third term as vice chairman. He has also served three years as a member of the Working Trials, Obedience and Agility Council.

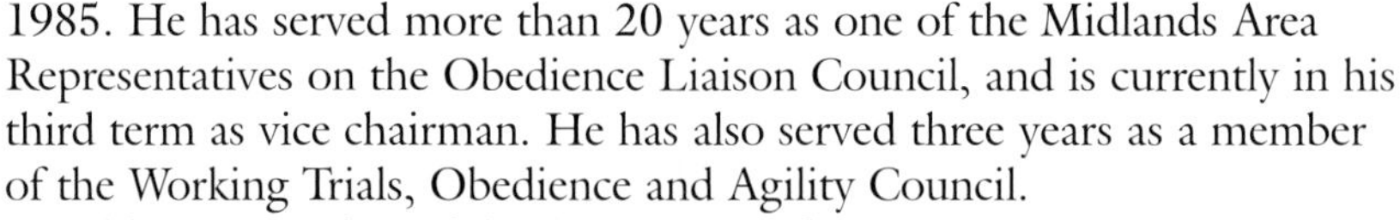

Paddy is a member of the Association of Pet Dog Trainers and a regular examiner for The Institute of Professional Dog Trainers. He was elected a full member of the Kennel Club in 1995.

Published by Ringpress Books

A Division of INTERPET Publishing

Vincent Lane, Dorking, Surrey RH4 3YX

Designed by Rob Benson

ISBN 1 86054 272 7

Printed and bound in Hong Kong through Printworks International

0 9 8 7 6 5 4 3 2 1

Contents

1 Getting Started

The ambition of all dog owners is to have a well-trained, obedient companion. That is no mean achievement, but training a dog to compete in Obedience takes something extra.

In fact, most handlers start in Competitive Obedience almost by accident. They start working with a puppy, and then get bitten by the bug, and make plans to test their skills at a higher level. Few handlers go out and choose a puppy specifically for Competitive Obedience. They do not think about finding out about a dog's genetic background, to enable selection of the right size and type of dog for the task. They will not have planned their own training by attending lectures, reading text books, and studying the top-flight teams in competition, prior to the dog's arrival – all of which is vital if you intend to compete against the best.

Many people start training, and then decide to test their skills at a higher level.

To a casual reader with no experience of working with people and animals, you might presume that such a start could never result in success. In fact, this is not the case. It seems that some people are born with a natural ability to work with, and get the best from, their dogs. This natural ability can be developed and honed with training and exposure to competition, but it cannot be purchased.

It is also true, as many of the sport's senior figures will readily confirm, that a clever and gifted dog (given a sporting chance) can work with a relatively poor handler to achieve top honours.

However, such extremes are rare. Most of us mere mortals will have some measure of natural ability, and will, in any case, massively benefit from and enjoy owning, looking after and training a dog. This, coupled with the pleasure and excitement generated from working in competition, will make all the hard work and time invested in training worthwhile.

Never frighten yourself by creating a one-sided balance sheet listing the time and expense necessary to achieve your chosen goal.

Get relations off to a good start by spending as much time as possible with your puppy.

It is equally important to counterbalance this with the exhilaration and pride you feel in the performance you achieve, and the sheer joy of owning a well-behaved, faithful dog.

A GOOD FOUNDATION

As stated, I am a great believer in spending time researching the background of your potential canine partner, and obtaining as much prior training (particularly hands-on) as possible. Future success or failure in competition will be greatly influenced by decisions made at this early stage.

Seek advice from people of standing in the canine world, and make sure you see the parents of the puppy you are considering purchasing. All puppies are cute, so be sure to follow your instincts and don't be scared to say 'no' if the puppy on offer is not for you, even if you can't fully explain why.

Having chosen your puppy, enjoy each other's company and make sure you bond by feeding, grooming and exercising your own dog – don't leave it to your partner or parents to do the hard work. He is your dog, and you must look after him.

LIVING IN THE REAL WORLD

Training for Competitive Obedience should be conducted throughout the dog's life. It should be in parallel with training the dog to become acceptable to the community in general, and your family and close neighbours in particular. In my opinion, success in competition is automatically cancelled out if the dog is a canine hooligan, and a nuisance to all.

A dog can be a top-flight competition winner and a canine good citizen – you do not have to choose one or the other, but you do have to train your dog for both.

Just as with top-flight sporting stars, success will only rarely come overnight, without hard work, endeavour and dedication – plus total respect for your canine partner.

However, do not lose heart if you do not achieve your ambitions in competition. You may not go home with too many rosettes, but you will be going home with your best and most faithful pal who will have done his best to please you. That is worth more than all the show awards wrapped up together.

PLAY TRAINING

Play training is probably the most effective way of communicating with your dog, and is the best way to start any form of training. Play should not stop once the dog has reached maturity; you should continue to teach, using this play method, during the whole of your dog's life.

I fully endorse the commonly held belief that, if you can play with your dog, you can train the dog. In the hands of an expert trainer, a dog will not realise he is being trained; he will assume it is all one big game. As a result, the dog will never become bored with his work. He will be happy to work, and always respond with enthusiasm for the task at hand.

If training is fun, a puppy will learn quickly and will never become bored.

It is useful, at this point, to consider what we mean by play. Just watch one of the wildlife programmes on television, and see how seriously lion or tiger cubs take a play session. The cubs use the play period to rehearse hunting moves that will be used in deadly earnest at another time. The training session is also used by the cubs to push and test the boundaries of what is acceptable behaviour in their dealings with litter brothers and sisters, or with other members of the pack.

Exercises, or more precisely exercises broken down into modules and component parts, should be practised and rehearsed with your dog until perfected during these play sessions. This is the best way of ensuring success when they are put together in competition. It is also the time when both dog and owner establish and cement the animal bond between them, and agree on boundaries of behaviour acceptable to each other.

Play training should continue throughout your dog's life.

The domestic dog is not a solitary animal and will always seek the company of others, in particular the company of the leader of the pack. As far as your dog is concerned, you are his leader. This does not mean that you are a stern disciplinarian, but you are the one with the better brain. Play sessions are fun for both you and your dog, and they are an important way of establishing and maintaining a balanced relationship between you and your dog.

2 Heelwork

To be successful in Obedience shows demands complete commitment from both members of the team. For the measured style of Heelwork needed in competition, it is essential for the dog's total, absolute and unfaltering attention to be focused on you. Some so-called pundits will waste your time disputing this, and pointlessly compare yesteryear's dream teams who worked to a different benchmark from today's high flyers. The reality is that, if you want to be successful, you must work to the standards of today.

At this juncture, it is worth stopping to consider the meaning of the word command. The dictionary definition is "to control" or "to order", and it is a term that we often associate with sergeant majors barking out commands to soldiers. This goes against the grain of the milder, reward-based training that is favoured today. But I think there is a middle way. There is no need to shout commands at your dog. Equally, you will make slow progress if you have to implore your dog to obey you. I am a great believer in making life as simple as I can for my dog. I am very positive and clear in giving precise commands, and ensuring my dog understands and obeys.

TEACHING "WATCH"

To start training this important base exercise, I sit my dog at my left side, in what is defined as the classical Heelwork position, and teach the command "*Watch*". To achieve a reaction to the word "*Watch*" while your dog is in the Sit position, you will need to attract his attention, using any of the methods developed during play sessions. You can use food, a play toy, or a clicker; you can click your fingers, talk to your dog, use eye contact, or a combination of several of the above.

This early training session should be kept to an absolute minimum, and finished when you have kept the dog's attention for just a few moments. Remember to give lots of reward for success in the early stages, and, in time, reduce the reward to a kind word. You will have to judge the appropriate level of reward for each individual training session for whatever exercise or part-exercise you are training your dog to do. We all work for wages or some sort of reward – so don't be a mean employer.

When your dog is responding to "*Watch*" for a few moments, the task is to develop this, in small stages. Work on the command over several training sessions until you have your dog's total attention for one minute. Keep repeating this until it can be supplied on demand.

FIRST STEPS

Now we can think about taking some steps of controlled Heelwork. I always train Heelwork on the lead, holding the lead over the dog's head, in my left hand.

Soft, rope leads are inexpensive, so cut one down to

TEACHING ATTENTION

A treat or toy can be used to focus the dog's attention.

Build up the exercise to develop your dog's concentration span.

The clicker has proved to be an effective means of teaching attention.

the exact size to facilitate Heelwork training. A lead that is too long is just a nuisance and delays the response time between fault and correction. In training, only relax lead control when teaching the positions on the move. To make the rope lead the correct length, sit the dog to heel with the lead attached, hold it in the desired position, mark it, and then cut to length.

When your dog is ready, start working on a few steps of attentive Heelwork.

- Command your dog to "Watch", and step forward (left leg first) no more than two or three steps, using a new command of *"Heel"*.
- Make sure the dog gives you total and absolute attention. If he is successful, be quick to give a reward.
- If you have not managed to keep the dog's attention, re-teach "Watch" and ensure you have total attention before attempting to step off.

These early stages of attentive Heelwork can take hours, or even days, to teach. It does not matter how long it takes to school your dog to *"Watch"*, it only matters that you and your dog are successful.

MAKING PROGRESS

Now we are able to progress to the precise Obedience

show style of Heelwork. This bears little resemblance to the type of Heelwork that is acceptable for walking the dog home from the park or shopping centre. But it is important to remember that in competition we are aiming for a standard of excellence, rather than basic good manners.

The dog is keeping his attention focused on you for a few steps of Heelwork, so now we must develop the exercise so that he will walk to heel in a straight line for some 50 paces. We can then progress to a large, left circle (anticlockwise), followed by a large right (or clockwise) circle.

Progress to working your dog in a circle.

The reason we progress to circles is that humans find it very difficult to walk in a straight line without some sort of artificial aid, and in attempting to do this we will inevitably create problems by walking into or away from our dogs.

At this stage, we have not introduced any other manoeuvres or distractions. In the words of the wise: "make haste slowly". It only matters that you teach the exercise correctly, not how quickly you complete this module. If, at any time, the dog gets distracted or loses interest, you are probably doing too much too quickly. Go back to the beginning and start to build this part of the exercise again, and take your time.

This basic, totally attentive Heelwork should be used as a warm-up or switch-on to work instruction, before performing in the show ring (or as a prerequisite of any training session or demonstration). Do not make this more complicated, and avoid chastising the dog, otherwise you will both go into the show ring feeling demoralised before you start.

If this exercise is used positively, it becomes a comforter to both the dog and the handler, similar to athletes stretching and limbering up to get ready for their event.

HEELWORK SIT

The next stage of Heelwork training is to sit the dog at the Heel position.

- You must give the "Sit" command at the moment your right foot is on the ground, and as your left foot comes in to meet the now stationary right foot. Bend your knees, keeping your back straight.
- Take the lead, now held in your right hand, up over the dog's head.
- Place the heel of the left hand over the rear of the dog's back, and point the fingers that are on the outside of the dog to act as a guide to sit the dog tight and straight against the foot.

The most common fault is that a handler will stop, and then try to sit the dog. The stop and the sit are one manoeuvre, and should be taught as one.

As the speed and accuracy of your dog's response becomes acceptable, ease off the extra aids: first the bending over and the use of a hand, then gradually the use of the lead to speed and position the Sit.

The disciplined placing of your feet will continue throughout your career in showing dogs in Obedience. Eventually, when competing in the higher classes, the position of your feet will be the only command or indication which tells the dog to sit.

When you are training, only be satisfied with a straight Sit, and never, ever accept second best. Again, make sure you over-reward in the early stages of training, and gradually reduce the quality of the reward in line with the level of the response.

On a daily basis, during your initial training warm-up, remind the dog, using all of the aids, of the speed and accuracy of the Sit.

Make sure you get a straight Sit – never be satisfied with second best.

FOOTWORK AND DEPORTMENT

The handler's footwork and deportment are crucial, and can well make the difference between winning first place and oblivion as an also-ran.

Before you continue with more advanced Heelwork training, you must ensure that your own personal standards of Heelwork and deportment are faultless.

- Are you walking at a speed to get your dog's attention without overexciting?
- Is your stride pattern correct to show the dog to his best advantage, or do you need to shorten or lengthen it?
- Are you consistent during every turn?
- Are you foot-perfect so that you turn using the same steps each time?
- Do you halt in the same way every time?

If the answer to any of these questions is '*no*', then you should not progress to advanced Heelwork training of your dog before perfecting your own work.

The use of a video camera, with instant playback facilities, can be of enormous help at this, or at any stage, of training. However, it is of particular value when conducting self-analysis. It is often difficult to take criticism from an observer – and many relationships have been tested in this way! Use a camera to record your work, and see the fault for yourself.

Your own personal footwork during the Heelwork section is critical in training and show-day performance. Watch any of the best combinations competing for top honours: the quality and consistency of footwork and general deportment is self-evident.

Both handlers and dogs have varied physical abilities, and so I find it almost impossible to lay down hard-and-fast rules for when and how to place each foot during every turn and manoeuvre. However, each move must be thought about and perfected in the first instance without a dog. Then, once the dog and handler are working happily as one, they must be honed and practised until both team members are foot-perfect each and every time they enter the show ring.

Good deportment is essential in Competitive Obedience.

The golden rules are:

- Look in the direction you intend to turn.
- Lead into any turn with the left foot.

RIGHT TURN

When your dog is performing totally attentive work (and not before), you can add a right turn to the repertoire.

- Give the command *"Close"*, preceded by the dog's name, and pointing the way with your left foot.
- Use a lead to gently guide the dog close to your left leg into, and during, the turn.
- When leaving the turn, again give the "Close" command. With the assistance of the lead, guide and keep the dog close, ensuring he does not drift away from your leg.
- In the early stages of training, after a few paces of Heelwork beyond the turn, break off training and be overindulgent in rewarding the dog.

Teaching the right turn.

No further turns or manoeuvres should be added until this right turn is perfected. A word of caution: do not give too many commands – you will not be able to give any in the show ring.

Chat to your dog to keep him happy; he won't understand the words, but, if the delivery is right, he will enjoy the tune.

ABOUT-TURN (RIGHT)

The next stage is to teach the complete about-turn. This

is where the time invested in learning and disciplining yourself to perform tight, consistent, controlled footwork will begin to pay dividends, so that you can now concentrate on helping and not confusing your dog. This would just not be possible if you had not accomplished and practised this manoeuvre before attempting to teach the dog.

- Use the command *"Close"* (as used for the right turn), preceded by the dog's name. Again, point the way into the turn with your left foot.
- As with the right turn, guide the dog around the complete turn with even finger pressure on the lead, ensuring the dog is as close as possible to the left leg.
- Give a command going into the turn, and repeat the command coming out of the turn.

Going into a right about-turn.

As discussed earlier, teach in play, and at all times keep the dog happy, to ensure keenness and the will to work. If your training is not going to plan, try to analyse the problem. Do not be too concerned if you have to revert to your earlier lessons. It is good practice to frequently remind your dog, applying basic training aids, to ensure accuracy and speed.

- In the early stages of training, break off teaching a few paces beyond the turn, and give your dog a really big reward. As soon as possible, reduce the quality and duration of the reward.

LEFT TURN

In my opinion, more marks are lost performing this turn in the Obedience ring than in any of the other manoeuvres. A different and careful approach needs to be taken in order to explain the requirement to the dog.

Teaching the left turn.

- Leave the dog attentively in the Sit. Go an arm's length away, turn left, and then take half a pace backwards.
- Pause, then call the dog (with the command *"Back"*), and almost simultaneously step forward, guiding the dog into close, attentive Heelwork.
- Repeat this phase of training until the dog accepts joining you and curving into your left leg.
- Now execute this turn during Heelwork. Use the command *"Back"*, and point the direction with your left foot. Use the lead and the calf of your left leg to gently turn the dog.

Do not over-practise one turn constantly, particularly the left turn. Dogs become bored and stale very quickly, and you risk becoming over-the-top with your rewards in an effort to motivate. This will result in the dog taking over, and he will most likely beat you into, and out of, every turn. It is far better not to bore the dog in the first place!

Make your Heelwork training varied, interesting and challenging and don't continue for long periods. In the lower classes, the Heelwork section of the test will only last two or three minutes, so the duration of your intense Heelwork training should reflect this short period of time.

As with all turns, the whole of the dog's body has to turn – not just the head. Once the dog becomes practised in this manoeuvre, contact with the left leg will disappear. You will then have to concentrate on keeping the dog close to your leg during the final stages of the turn, and, critically, immediately after turning.

Two of the major faults are: only the dog's head turning, and the opposite i.e. the dog over-turning. You may be unaware of these problems when training, which emphasises the need for a training partner to assist and help you. Re-teach the exercise module from the beginning and make sure of total accuracy before moving on.

LEFT ABOUT-TURN

Do not attempt to teach this turn before you have perfected the left turn. As the right about-turn is an extension to the right turn, so the left about-turn is an extension to the left turn.

To gain maximum points in competition, you have to enter and exit this turn on an imaginary straight line. Possibly, like me, you will find this difficult in an open outdoor training area, without some form of aid.

To start my schooling, I use two poles, and tie a light rope to each so that the rope is lying taut on the ground. As I become more competent, I use three poles and a light rope to form one corner of a practice show ring. As a point of interest, this set-up is used to school many of the moves used in Heelwork and other exercises. I only rarely erect a complete ring when teaching, as I find it inhibiting and restrictive.

A reminder before you attempt the left about-turn with your dog: make sure your own footwork is rehearsed until it is automatic, polished and totally consistent.

- As for the left turn, command *"Back"*, and point the way into the turn with your left foot.
- Using your left arm, guide the dog with the lead, and verbally encourage him. Do not bend over the dog during the turn; it is important to maintain an upright posture.
- Walk a straight line, and, if necessary, attempt to walk through your dog. Obviously, the dog will move out of your way, and will respond to your positive lead.
- Watch out for the dog going wide after the turn.
- In the early stages of training, move a few paces on from the left about-turn, and then go into raptures

Heelwork with dog and handler in a perfect position.

and over-reward your dog. Just as importantly, progress towards reducing your reward to a few kind words at the end of the particular move, or when you have completed your training session.

PUPPY RECALL

The practice of teaching a young or inexperienced dog the Recall at the same time as Heelwork has multiple benefits.

PUPPY RECALL

This exercise can be used for inexperienced dogs, or simply as a means of breaking up an intensive period of Heelwork.

1. Walking to heel, prior to the command to "Come front".

2. The dog is called in as the handler backs off.

Three of the more important are:

❶ It teaches the dog to react and respond to his name.
❷ It teaches the dog the front Recall into the Present position, without spoiling the ongoing Stay training.
❸ It can be used to break up intensive Heelwork, or, paradoxically, it can be used to regain attention if a dog is distracted.

In preparation, attach a full lead to your dog's collar and launch into a normal Heelwork training session.

- Call your dog's name. At this point, the dog is required to respond and look towards his handler for instruction (as you would react if you heard your own name being called at home or at work).
- If the dog fails to respond to the call, repeat his name, and give a slight jerk on the lead. Carry on with your Heelwork, and call his name until he responds in the prescribed manner. Today, we are going to ask the dog to perform the Recall. In future, the dog's name is going to be used as a prerequisite to a whole host of commands, so a response to the name in early teaching is paramount.
- Give the dog the command *"Come front"*, and encourage the dog to come to you. Trot backwards, encouraging the dog to come closer and closer. Once he is within a few inches/cms of your legs, stop and sit the dog straight in front.
- Once the dog has sat, keep his attention on you. Count to ten, and then give a big reward. When appropriate, reduce the intensity and excitement of the recompense.

CHANGING PACE

Variation and changes of pace should be introduced as soon as possible in a dog's career. Do not wait until you have qualified out of lower competition, and are a few short weeks away from contesting a higher level.

In the initial stages, training for changes of pace will be started as an extension to left and right circle work. They will add diversity and variety to your daily training routine. As with training for normal pace, turns and halts will not be introduced until total perfection of varying pace is achieved.

SLOW PACE

To the uninitiated, Heelwork at slow pace would appear to be easy – but this is not so. For the handler, the problem lies in keeping your balance and maintaining stride pattern, both of which are crucial to ensure perfect Heelwork.

It helps if you move your point of balance back by adopting more of a squat posture, in preference to an upright walk-tall type position. This will enable you to have a longer stride, and will greatly assist when encountering uneven surfaces.

In the Obedience ring, slow pace only occurs in the more advanced classes. The requirements stipulate

Slow pace: Dogs are very sensitive to body language, and this is especially true when introducing a change of pace.

that the handler is not allowed to speak to the dog without penalty (other than to command the dog when stepping off from the halt).

I have already stated that training should commence for this pace at an early stage, but to do so without verbal encouragement would be counterproductive, and would very quickly destroy a dog's confidence. Each dog is different and has varying needs, so you, as the real expert on your own dog, will have to make a judgement as to when the dog is ready to perform slow pace as stipulated in the Obedience ring.

In training, I am always prepared to chat to a dog when necessary, varying the words as much as possible so as not to be repetitive. The dog will not understand all the words, but if you use the right tone it will be beneficial. Limit the number of commands used, but, at the same time, teach key words like "Sit", "Close", or "Heel".

A dog is far more responsive to body language than to verbal commands, so restrict the barrage of instructions delivered in boring monotones, and replace it with warmth and encouragement. At no time is this more relevant than in slow pace. In the early stages of teaching, start from the halt, and only continue for a few paces (as for our earlier training for normal pace).

Changing from slow pace to normal pace is accomplished by taking a longer stride with your left leg, and helping the dog to maintain position with a lead. Initially, you will also give an appropriate verbal command. The more difficult manoeuvre is to change from normal pace to slow pace. However, the technique used is exactly the same.

It is of paramount importance that the handler performs both changeovers without any hesitation, effortlessly and smoothly. Again, I would advise the handler to practise without a dog and to be foot-perfect before working with a dog. Take advice from your training coach/partner as to the best stride pattern to suit your dog. Again, the use of a video camera with an instant playback facility, is of great benefit in establishing this.

The dog must not falter or mark time; he must appear to glide over the ground. Generally, most handlers will walk with a longer stride to obtain the best from their dogs. Study the opposition – particularly the 'in-form' teams who are doing all the winning – it's surprising what you can learn from watching others.

FAST PACE

As for the other two paces, you will need to study your stride pattern to ensure that optimum performance is achieved. In reality, the vast majority of dogs get a real buzz from performing fast pace, so problems are more likely to arise because a dog is hyped up. Controlled fast pace is achievable without flattening your dog's performance, or getting him overexcited.

Start from the halt, and initially trot only slightly faster than the speed at which you walk. With a fully trained dog, do not practise long stretches of more than 50 or 60 paces without reverting to half a dozen or so paces of

Fast pace: Dogs enjoy working at this pace, so you must be careful not to allow your dog to become overexcited.

normal Heelwork. If you have a beginner/novice dog, limit the amount of fast pace still further.

In the first part of a Heelwork training session (and always in your warm-up session before entering the ring), keep close control with the use of a short lead and tight verbal control. Keep calm, a display of annoyance on your part will only disrupt concentration, and generally spoil the bond between both team members.

Fast pace can be used as a wake-up for dogs losing attention in normal or slow Heelwork. However, make sure you do not spoil your hard work by finishing off every Heelwork training session (whatever the pace), by using a session of fast work to overexcite and reward your dog.

When starting to teach fast pace, as for early training in normal pace, perfect the performance over a straight line of some 50 paces, and then add a left and right circle. When you have achieved a satisfactory standard, add the Sit position. It is best in the early stages of training to add turns (right, left or about) after just six or so paces, when you are most likely to have complete, close control. The turns to be tested at a show are restricted to left, right and about-turn, and, in the most advanced class, dog and handler may be asked to perform complete multiple turns, weaves or a circle.

POSITIONS ON THE MOVE

In the advanced class, the handler is required to Sit, Stand and Down their dog during normal Heelwork. The handler is only allowed to use the dog's name, and one single verbal command or a signal. These positions *must* only be taught to a dog who is working confidently – although do not wait until he is working in the higher classes.

It is important to make a judgement that the dog is self-assured and working happily in all three paces. The handler must have decided how to instruct the dog, and be totally foot-perfect before attempting the positions with their dog.

So as not to confuse your dog, train one position at a time, and, even with an experienced dog, make a point of not practising too frequently. There is no need to practise all three positions in one training session. If you feel you must, then perform some slow and fast Heelwork between each position. At all costs, avoid having a well-intentioned but misguided person spooking your dog, by barking instructions at you. The only assertive instruction to perform positions on the move should come from a ring steward on show day.

You, the handler, need to have it firmly fixed in your mind that you will always carry out positions on the move with great care and understanding, keeping your composure at all times. Oppressive over-correction of a missed position or a minor mistake can take ages to compensate for. It is much better to remain level-headed and in control.

I advocate the use of a light rope lead cut down (or made specially) to size for tight control during Heelwork training, and I consider such a lead an absolute must for the initial training of positions on the move.

SIT

Start off by teaching Sit on the move.

- In the course of your Heelwork, halt in what is by now the frequent, well-practised technique.
- Pause for a split second, commanding your dog to remain sitting, and then walk a complete left circle with the training lead in your left hand, positioned over the dog's head.
- Watch your dog at all times.
- Speak to your dog to ensure confidence, and stop when you have completed the circle with the dog at your left side.
- After a pause of a couple of seconds, use the command *"Heel"*, and continue forward together some six paces before over-rewarding your dog.
- Work on this position, gradually reducing the stopping time beside the dog.
- Then gradually extend the circle, first placing the lead on the dog's back.

ON THE MOVE: SIT

1. The dog is commanded to Sit.

2. After a pause of a couple of seconds, continue with normal heelwork.

- Develop and vary the pattern of Heelwork you do, but be in position to watch your dog and give words of encouragement or a command to Sit if needed.
- Finally, pick up the dog in Heelwork with a single command and without a pause, when reaching the working side.

A word of warning: do not overpractise any of the Heelwork positions, as this will introduce hesitation into the Heelwork itself.

The exercise of walking in a circle around your dog has many benefits. For example, the dog can be seen at all times, you will know what he is doing without looking over your shoulder (another cause of hesitation), and it can also be used as an aid to discourage forward movement.

STAND

Teach the Stand next, but I would suggest that you avoid using the full word of command *"Stand"*, and simply use the latter part of the word – *"And"*. If you attempt to use the full word, a bright, keen dog will have sat long before the whole word has been spoken. Other words of command can be used like "Up", or you can rely on a hand signal.

- The initial Stand should be taught with your right hand in the dog's collar. Walk the dog in a small right circle, touch the stifle joint with the left hand and command the dog "And". After a pause of several seconds, reward the dog.
- Continue in this way until you can command the dog to *Stand* without touching the dog with your left hand, and using a lead instead of holding the collar.
- As with the Sit position, place the dog into position during Heelwork.
- After a few seconds' pause, walk in a left circle around the dog, holding the lead in your left hand, positioned over the dog's head. Give plenty of reassurance.
- Stand beside the dog for a few seconds, and then continue forward together with a command of *"Heel"*.
- Develop the exercise, placing the lead on the dog's back, and extending the circle, adding variation to the Heelwork.
- Finally pick the dog up, without any hesitation, with a command *"Heel"*, and continue forward for six or so paces before rewarding your dog.

ON THE MOVE: STAND

1. Leave the dog in the Stand.

2. The handler returns, walking past the dog.

3. The dog is collected.

4. Dog and handler continue with normal Heelwork.

ON THE MOVE: DOWN

1. The dog is commanded to drop.

2. The handler leaves the dog in the Down.

DOWN

Finally, teach the Down position. An instant Down is a prerequisite to teaching this move.

- Start by walking with your dog beside you, with the training lead attached to his collar
- Give the dog the command *"Down"*, and place your dog into position using the lead to speed the drop and reinforcing the Down with your left hand on the dog's shoulder.

- As with the previous two positions, pause beside your dog, and then walk a small circle with the lead held over the dog's head, reassuring your dog at all times. Develop and vary the Heelwork you do while the dog is down.
- When you return to the working side of the dog, pause for a second and give the command *"Heel"*, and continue forward together for half a dozen strides before rewarding your dog.

Develop and nurture all three positions until they can be executed with an immediate response to the word of command. The dog must remain in position until, without any anticipation, he is commanded to join the handler, making instant contact and continuing in flowing Heelwork.

3 Stays

When you are competing, you have no option but to complete the Stay exercises in the order dictated by the judge. Depending on the level of the test, you may be asked to do the 'Stand Stay' first followed by the 'Sit Stay' and finally the 'Down Stay'.

In my training routine, I rarely practise more than one Stay position a day with an experienced dog. I never, under any circumstances, practise more than one position per day with a young, inexperienced or confused dog.

SIT STAY

To start this exercise, the dog must sit at your left side, looking upright and alert. In the initial training, we first make sure the dog is upright by calling him into the Present position, as used for the puppy Recall during Heelwork.

Check that the 'D' ring on the dog's collar is at the top of his neck, and attach a one-metre (3-ft) lead.

Training the Sit Stay.

- Place the lead over the back of your left wrist, and step back to the working side of the dog.
- Command your dog to *"Stay Sit"*, step forward, leading with your right foot, and walk about one and a half paces away from the dog.
- Half-face your dog, and open your left hand as a signal to reinforce the Sit command. If the dog attempts to move, raise the lead over his head and repeat the command "*Sit*".
- After three or four seconds, return to the working side of the dog. At the same time, funnel the lead into your right hand ready to enforce the Sit. Count to three, and praise the dog.
- Gradually increase the time you stand in front of the dog. Once you can be in front of the dog for more than a minute, stop placing the lead over your wrist, but do maintain your hand signal.
- You can now increase the time you can leave your dog in stages until a Stay of two minutes' duration can be easily accomplished.
- Next, remove the lead, and gradually build up the Sit Stay by starting with a Stay of a few seconds, increasing to a few minutes, and then dispensing with the hand signal.
- If, at any time, you hit failure, start your training from the beginning and build the dog's confidence by carefully and successfully completing each stage.

Do not be concerned about repeating earlier training. It is important to take your time, and to teach correctly for long-term soundness and dependability.

The St(AND) Stay is being taught using a toy.

ST(AND) STAY

I have found that a high proportion of my pupils insist on making this exercise over-complicated and fussy, despite the fact that standing must be about the most natural position for any breed of dog.

- Hold the dog's collar with your right hand (you do not need a lead for this exercise). Step forward so you can stretch and stand the dog, touching the stifle joint with the index finger of your left hand.
- Use your right hand (which is also holding the collar), and gently tickle the dog's neck.
- Use a soothing tone of voice and command the dog to *"And"*. You will notice that I have deliberately dropped the "St" from the command word *"Stand"*. A smart, keen dog will be well on his way to sitting by the time you have delivered the first part of the complete word, and a slow dog will just end up being confused.
- If you are training a small to medium-sized dog, you can put him on a table or bench to teach this exercise. This puts dog and handler on the same level, so you are not too overbearing or dominant by looming above him. With larger breeds, you cannot use a table,

so you must be aware of your body language in order to avoid bending over or dominating the dog from above.

- Once your dog will happily stand beside you, move an arm's length to the side. Make sure you remain close enough to correct the dog if necessary.
- Increase the time you are standing away from the dog by five-second intervals until the duration of the Stand is one minute, and you are several paces from your dog.
- Now build the exercise until you can walk within the peripheral vision of your dog, returning at intervals to gently reassure and praise.
- Finally, as required when competing in the show ring, stand with your back to the dog and gradually increase the length of the Stay to a period of one minute.

Take your time and teach in stages. Do not be tempted to cut out some of the steps, and, in the process, ruin all your hard work. Remember, the dog must be confident in the knowledge that he is pleasing his handler.

DOWN STAY

The first stages of this exercise can be taught in one of your indoor play sessions.

- In the first instance, it might be helpful to use a food treat to persuade the dog to go into the Down position. Lure your dog into position, commanding *"Down"*, and then stay squatting by the side of your dog.

Start by using a food treat to lure the dog into the Down.

A word of caution: I am very careful about how I reward my dogs at the end of any of the Stay exercises. Be calm and controlled, and resist the temptation of being over-exuberant. In the show ring, it is not acceptable to be over-the-top and noisy when rewarding your dog for completing a Stay exercise. It is all too easy to upset other exhibitors and their dogs who are competing close by, or sharing the ring with you.

- When your dog is responding to the "Down" command, increase the time he stays in position by five- or ten-second stages until you can easily reach two minutes.

- Now start from the beginning, only this time slowly stand up and move one or two paces away from your dog. In the early learning stages, keep returning and reassuring him.
- Now move outdoors and teach the exercise from the start. If taught correctly, the outdoor training will have a very rapid conclusion.

As with the other Stay exercises, take your time and do not progress the training until each stage produces solid and positive results. Do not worry if you have to go back a couple of stages and reinforce your training – it will probably produce better long-term results.

Last command: Practise Stays in different positions to boost confidence.

OUT OF SIGHT

If your Stay exercises have been taught with due care in the prescribed manner, then a Stay out of sight should only be considered as an extension to your earlier training programme.

- In the early stages, teach the exercises on your home territory so that your dog feels completely confident. Only go a short distance away so that you can still see your dog, and reinforce your command if necessary.
- Build the time you spend out of sight in fifteen-second stages until you achieve three or more minutes.
- Now work on the longer Down Stay, increasing minute by minute until you achieve the required time.
- To ensure dependability and stability in your training for the extended Down Stay, initially make a habit of returning to your dog every two or three minutes. You can give reassurance, without breaking

In time, your dog will be confident enough to stay with other dogs when you are out of sight.

the exercise, and then go out of sight again.
- Once the out of sight Stays are being performed to your satisfaction at home, move to a new, safe location, and carefully repeat all the stages of training.

In time, your dog will be ready to join other mature dogs whose out of sight Stays are absolutely solid. This will provide further practice to develop and secure all three Stay exercises before you are ready to progress to the show ring.

GOING WRONG

Keen observers of fellow competitors will often see that a particular handler always has a problem with the Stay exercises, regardless of the dog they are competing with. The handler seems to be blissfully unaware that they themselves might be an underlying cause of the problem.

There are several reasons for this on-going record of failure, but this is my favourite theory. Stays at a show are performed as a group exercise, and most people who are members of a training club will make a point of training Stays in this way. This is all very laudable if it is successfully accomplished, but, if it is unsuccessful, it is a disaster!

Take the example of Mr/Mrs Unsuccessful (above) owner of several dogs, all of whom are proving unreliable in Stays.

- Have they been taught individually?
- Have they been correctly set up for the test?

- Have they been taught one Stay exercise only per day?
- Have they left the practice ring at the dog club after completing one Stay exercise of the handler's choice?

I don't think so. The most likely scenario is that all the dogs from the owner's kennel have been used to practise a group Stay, and the king or queen pack leader has broken the Stays on a regular basis. The other dogs have followed this example, and they are now all totally confused.

The lesson is: train one dog at a time, and one Stay exercise at a time. *Never* train a dog in sight or within the hearing of any of your other dogs. Tell one dog off, and the other suffers. Equally, if you praise one dog, the other also is rewarded, regardless of what he is doing at the time.

4 Recall And Finish

As stated in earlier sections, care should be taken not to start teaching a formal Recall before your dog's Stays are totally consistent and dependable.

FRONT RECALL

This exercise should be introduced during play sessions. The handler sits on the floor with legs stretched out to form a channel. The dog, in play, is then called along this pathway to sit centrally and straight – with not too many options.

This can be developed with the handler sitting on a chair, and the dog is called to sit between the feet, with the legs used to ensure he is both central and straight.

Remember that during our Heelwork training, the dog is also being taught the rudimentary puppy Recall (see page 27).

- Sit the dog and give the command to *"Sit and Wait"*.
- Oozing total and absolute confidence, step sideways and away from the dog, and go to the end of a long lead. Face the dog, commanding him to *"Sit"*, if necessary.
- After a pause of at least 10 seconds, call the dog to you with the command *"Front"*. The dog should come to you at a trot, and sit centrally and straight.

PLAY RECALL

1. Sit on the floor, and use your legs as a channel to encourage your dog to come in to you.

2. The dog comes in and sits straight.

- If you have followed earlier advice (see puppy Recall), trotting backwards at this stage will certainly speed the approach.

Once the dog has sat in front of you, do not, under any circumstances, move and hassle the dog if you consider the Sit is not accurate. It is better to encourage the dog to adopt a central alignment while he is on the move.

If all else fails, reposition yourself at the last nanosecond so the dog finds the obligatory spot to sit and thinks he has sat straight.

Once the dog is performing happily, stand your ground and let the dog come to you. In some cases, it can be helpful to use food as a lure. If you decide to do this, hold the reward in both hands centrally, and high enough to ensure the dog raises his head to taste. Try not to use tiny portions of food treats as a reward, but, if necessary, use one treat in each hand so the dog is kept guessing.

Do not let the dog get lazy or over-demanding when using food as a reward, and, just like any form of reward, reduce to just a kind word as soon as possible.

When training, do not habitually finish, or give praise and reward, at this juncture. Pause for at least five seconds, walk around your dog, and end with the dog in the classical Heel position. In the early stages, make sure you give a really big reward at this stage.

Progress your teaching until the exercise can be produced off the lead and at will.

FRONT RECALL

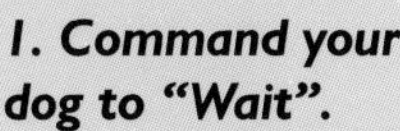

1. Command your dog to "Wait".

2. Turn and face the dog.

3. Call the dog in.

4. The dog comes into the front Present position.

FINISH

(Send the dog to heel)

When you are in the early stages of teaching the front Recall, do not send your dog to heel. Even with an advanced dog, only ask for an occasional Finish (not more than one in four). The obvious exception is in competition, when you will be told to *"Finish"*, and you will be expected to send the dog to heel, either to your left or right.

When training from the Present position, the handler should keep the dog guessing by varying what comes next. It could be one of the following:

- Sending the dog to heel (left or right).
- Stepping left to the working side of the dog.
- Walking to the right, and all the way around, to the working side.
- Breaking the exercise with praise from the initial Present position.

LEFT FINISH

During the initial training stages, attach a standard lead to your dog's collar and sit the dog in the conventional working position close to your left leg.

- In preparation for a practice Finish, step to the front of your dog, placing yourself into the Present position. Make sure the ring on the dog's collar is below and at the centre of the dog's chin.
- With an appropriate command (mine is *"Round")*, hold the lead in your left hand and (without bending) step back with the left leg.

LEFT FINISH

1. Start in the Present position, and give a command, such as "Round", to finish.

2. The handler steps back, using hand, lead and leg in unison.

3. The dog turns inwards.

4. Back at the handler's side.

- Use the lead to guide and direct, moving the dog behind and to your side.
- Turn the dog inwards, and, with the left leg, take a small step forward, to sit the dog straight and in the working position.
- Count to three and praise the dog.

The initial use of the left hand is developed so that it can be used in conjunction with the dog's name as a signal, plus the verbal command to heel (you will have to decide which is best for your dog, hand signal or verbal command, before competing in the higher classes).

After performing the Finish a few times, and when the dog is readily responding, start to reduce the extra aids until only a hand combined with a verbal command is left.

Most of the aids are applied for the first Finish of any training session only when the dog is reminded of the need for total and absolute accuracy.

Now, from the beginning, repeat and add polish to the whole process – only this time with the dog off the lead.

RIGHT FINISH

As for the previous left Finish, the lead is attached and we start with the dog in the conventional Heel position.

- The handler steps forward into the Present position.
- Thread the lead behind you, holding the handle in your left hand and a section close to the clip in your

RIGHT FINISH

1. The command to finish is given with the dog in the Present.

2. The handler steps back with the right leg to guide the dog.

3. The handler gives a small step forwards to encourage the dog to go round.

4. Going into the Sit.

5. Exercise finished.

right hand (exactly where depends on the size of your dog).

- Give the dog an appropriate command (mine is *"Heel")*, and pass the lead behind you, from your right hand into your left, guiding and encouraging the dog to be close. The use of your right hand develops a hand signal that can be used in conjunction with the dog's name (See page 42).
- Once more, sit the dog straight and accurately at your left side. If necessary, during the early stages of learning, swap the lead to your right hand, taking it up over the dog's head. To sit the dog, use the left hand on the dog's rear and side.
- Once this move is perfected and readily produced on demand, take the dog off the lead and practise the

I have yet to meet the partnership that can perform either the left or the right Finish with equivalent proficiency. One Finish will, on a regular and routine basis, be stronger and more reliable.

When teaching, you must continue to practise both, but, if you are competing at a show, use the Finish that you, or more importantly that the judge, will consider the best.

A restricted training session, with the dog on the lead and concerted aids with assistance, is not a detrimental step, but a return to basics. This acts as a comfort and reminds the dog of the precise requirements of the module being undertaken. As such, it should be repeated on a regular basis.

whole process, repeating and perfecting ready for show-day performance.

RECALL TO HEEL

In common with most people who train dogs for any of the working disciplines, my training lead has an 'O' ring as a component part of the handle. In order to extend this lead ready to train for this exercise, I simply clip a second lead on to it.

- Attach the extended lead on to your dog's collar, and sit the dog in the classical working position straight against your left leg.
- Command the dog to *"Wait"* and walk forward to almost the end of the extended lead.
- Stop, turn left, and take a couple of steps back. You are now in a position to call your dog, who will be within your range of vision.
- Call your dog, using his name, followed by the command *"Heel"*. Walk forward, using the extended lead to guide the dog into position.
- Continue walking forward for several paces of quality Heelwork. And praise your dog. Do not introduce halts or turns at this stage; they only slow and confuse the dog.
- Continue to train in this manner until you can walk in different directions, with as many halts and turns as you wish, *before* you call. Again, do not introduce halts or turns at this stage of training *after* you have called the dog.

RECALL TO HEEL

1. Leave the dog, stepping off on the right foot.

2. The handler follows the steward's instructions.

3. The dog remains in the Sit until commanded to Heel.

4. The dog rejoins his handler.

5. Dog and handler continue in normal Heelwork.

- When you call, ensure that you are in a position where you can see the dog's performance, and can encourage him to walk briskly to your left side. The dog should not just amble in to catch you up, or arrive like a steam train and knock you flying!
- Remove the extended lead and practise the stages as above until the exercise is perfect.
- Sits and turns are taught in Heelwork, and there should be no need to train them during a Recall. You can add them in on occasion, but this is purely a measure to reassure the handler.

When competing at the shows, in most classes you will have your back to, and be walking away from, your dog, before calling him and continuing forward together. It would be nonsense to train your dog with your eyes shut, and it is equally impractical to train with your back to your dog.

At all times when training, make sure you are totally aware of your dog's position and behaviour. This will only serve to enhance your dog's show-day performance.

5 Retrieve

The starting point of this exercise is play. Regardless of the age of the dog, the Retrieve must be taught as a game. Get down on the floor, or sit on a low chair, and play with a toy – this can be a favourite plaything, or you can use an old glove or a piece of rag. The object is to get the dog interested in the 'retrieve article'. Let the dog pull it or chase it. Try to motivate your dog to run after it, and bring it back for more fun.

Whatever you do, do not reprimand your dog, as this will kill his enthusiasm. I am writing this with my 14-year-old Border Collie dropping a ball on my foot and begging me to have a game. If your dog has not enjoyed the benefit of structured play and the enjoyment of the chase prior to the formality and the high degree of accuracy required in perfecting this exercise, then do not attempt to teach this module. The prerequisite of a formal Retrieve is play and yet more play. The dog will also be required to perform a front Recall.

RETRIEVE A DUMBBELL

PHASE 1

- With the lead attached, sit your dog in the working position at your left side.

HOLDING THE DUMBBELL

1. The dog is commanded to hold the dumbbell.

2. The dog holds the dumbbell for a few moments.

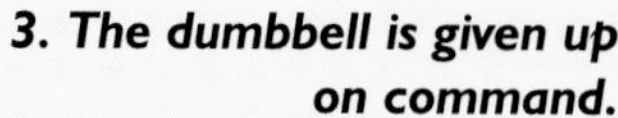

3. The dumbbell is given up on command.

- Open the dog's mouth with the fingers of your left hand. Hold the end of the dumbbell (not the shaft) with the extended fingers of your right hand, and place the bell in the dog's mouth with a command *"Hold"*.
- After a delay of about 20 seconds, take the dumbbell from the dog's mouth with the single command *"Give"*.
- If the dog lets go without a command, place the dumbbell back in the mouth with a further command *"Hold"*. After a pause of several seconds, repeat the *"Give"* command, and then take the dumbbell.
- Repeat the first stages from above until the dog readily opens his mouth when the dumbbell is offered, and holds it without chewing or mouthing. When commanded to *"Give"*, the dog must open his mouth and release the dumbbell into your hand.

Take care not to gallop ahead and spoil your good work by advancing to the next stage too quickly. It is much better to take your time (days) and make sure the first stages of teaching the exercise are solid and can be reliably repeated without any problems. Keep your dog happy and remember to praise and reward.

PHASE 2

- Hold the end of the dumbbell (not the shaft) with the fingers of your right hand. Place the dumbbell just below the line of the dog's mouth, and in front of your body.

HOLDING THE DUMBBELL

1. Hold the dumbbell in front of you.

2. Encourage the dog to come round to hold the dumbbell.

- Take the dog from your side to the dumbbell using the *"Hold"* command. If you have taught the first stages correctly, the dog will open his mouth to hold the dumbbell.
- Back off until the dog is facing you. Take the dumbbell with the command *"Give"* (before the dog sits), and then praise and reward.
- Repeat and advance the training until your dog will hold the dumbbell, and sit in front of you, before giving up the bell on command.

Again, teach and practise over several days until this stage of the dog's training is totally reliable. The dog should happily repeat and enjoy this exercise. By now you know my philosophy – "teach the early stages in play and over-reward early learning".

PHASE 3

- With the dog sitting at your left side, hold the dumbbell in your right hand and drop the bell on the ground an arm's length in front of you.
- Give your dog the command *"Hold"*. At the same time, step forward with your left leg, placing your foot beyond the bell, moving and encouraging the dog to go round your foot, to face you before picking up the bell.

HOLDING THE DUMBBELL

1. Place the dumbbell in front of you.

2. Encourage the dog to come round to hold the dumbbell.

- Back off and repeat your earlier training with the dog sitting in front, and giving up the dumbbell on the command "*Give*". Then praise and reward your dog.

PHASE 4

- Sit the dog at your left side, and, for the first time, remove the lead.
- Command the dog to "*Wait*", and throw the dumbbell about 8-10 feet in front of you in a straight line.
- Send the dog out to retrieve with a command "*Hold*". Follow the dog out, and encourage him to pick up the dumbbell quickly and cleanly.
- Trot back, stopping for the dog to sit in front and present the dumbbell for you to take with the command "*Give*".
- Perform a Finish of your choice.
- After a sensible pause (i.e. count to three), reward your dog and congratulate yourself – you have done well!

The principal aim of Phase 3 is to ensure the dog goes around the back of the dumbbell before picking it up. This promotes a smooth, clean pick-up, and eliminates knocking the dumbbell on, or scrambling in a hectic rush to get hold of it. Practise and repeat, keeping the dog happy and keen at all times. This phase of training will be used throughout a dog's career as a precursor to retrieve.

TEACHING THE RETRIEVE

1. Throw the dumbbell.

2. The dog is encouraged to come in.

3. Returning to the handler.

4. In the Present position so the handler can take the dumbbell.

5. Most important of all – the reward!

PHASE 5

- Sit the dog at your left side, without a lead.
- Throw the dumbbell out in a straight line, about 10-12 feet in front.
- With a single command of *"Hold"*, send the dog out.
- Verbally encourage the dog to hold the dumbbell and return to you.
- With the dog sitting in front of you, take the dumbbell with the command *"Give"*.
- Perform a Finish of your choice, and then praise and reward your dog.

Remember, the main aim is for the dog to retrieve a dumbbell. Do not spoil your Retrieve by chastising and nagging for any faults that are associated with a Recall; they are to be cured and corrected at the proper time – when training the front Recall.

In Retrieve practice sessions, avoid the dog anticipating the Finish element of this exercise by only performing a conventional Finish on rare occasions.

RETRIEVE OTHER ARTICLES

With a new type of retrieve article, the training pattern will be:

- Introduce in a play-training period several days before a Retrieve practice.
- Sit the dog beside you, off-lead. Offer the article to the dog with the command *"Hold"*. If necessary, open the dog's mouth and gently insert the article. Do not

HOLDING DIFFERENT ARTICLES

In the advanced classes, the dog must retrieve an article that is chosen by the judge.

progress beyond this point until the dog is readily accepting the article from you.

- With the dog sitting beside you, throw the article in front of you (10-12 feet).
- Send the dog out with a command of *"Hold"*, and run out after the dog, encouraging him to pick up the item cleanly.
- Trot back, stopping to take the article from your dog when he is sitting in front of you.
- Finally, practise as if working a test at the show. Only train the complete exercise rarely; it is much better to keep the dog playful, keen, and willing to participate.

You should only need to apply the above full training routine to an article that is totally dissimilar to anything the dog has retrieved before.

Beware of dirty articles and items with a strong smell as they can put a dog off very easily, destroying weeks of hard work. You must also be aware of the effect temperature may have on an item: cold metal will stick to a dog's lips and gums, and the effect of hot metal on a dog's mouth needs no explanation. An increase or decrease in temperature will also strongly influence the smell of some objects. Feel and smell the article yourself, and, if in any doubt, do not use the item.

If you are asked to use an item in competition that you do not consider suitable, or that might cause your dog distress, walk away without competing and think of the detrimental effect it might have on your dog's future career.

6 Send Away

If we ignore the Drop and Recall elements of the exercise, the requirement is to send the dog in the direction indicated by the judge. In reality, the dog is generally expected to go to a single or a combination of markers of various colours, sizes and shapes, before being instructed to lie down.

This has to be the basis of our training: to perform to the typical test set by the vast majority of mainstream judges, and to ignore the extremely rare occasion when we are asked to upset our dogs and spoil earlier training because of a one-off, nonconformist test.

You need a happy, confident dog for a successful Send Away.

The accuracy of the Send Away required in modern Obedience has to be inch-perfect, and all early training should reflect this.

As with teaching any other exercises, it is preferable to break the Send Away into smaller, separate stages. Each stage should be repeated and perfected over days before moving on to the next. Even if you have an experienced dog, performing a complete Send Away, with new, unfamiliar target markers, should be reserved for competition. In training, it is much better to provide as much help and assistance as necessary to achieve a successful Send Away with a happy, confident dog.

DROP ON COMMAND

STAGE 1 OF 3

- Start teaching this exercise in early play sessions. Sit on the ground with your dog on a lead. Point to the ground and put the dog into position with the "Down" command. Teach in a light-hearted, playful manner, and follow it up with lots and lots of fuss. The dog will very quickly join in the game and will willingly drop into the Down for praise and fuss.
- When the dog will drop with just a single command, progress to stage two.

Take great care not to be heavy-handed with a young puppy, and force him into a Down position. A youngster who is under six or seven months has green, flexible bones that can be damaged.

STAGE 2 OF 3

- Walk with your dog on the lead, and, after taking several steps, point to the ground and give the *"Down"* command. At the same time, use the lead to reinforce the position. Continue in this way, encouraging and helping the dog to go down quickly.
- If you are meeting undue resistance, go back over earlier training and remind the dog in a play period what the Down is all about.
- Progress this stage until your dog will drop promptly, with a single command and no additional aids.

STAGE 3 OF 3

Ask a trusted training partner to assist you for this stage.

- Your partner walks your dog, on a lead, away from you. When they are about 7-10 feet away, use the dog's name to get his attention, and point to the ground, giving the *"Down"* command.
- At this stage, the training partner will help and encourage the dog to drop into position, but without speaking to the dog.
- Once the dog is down, run out to reward him with lots and lots of praise.
- Extend the distance and repeat the routine. Once the dog has gained in confidence, the training partner will be able to greatly reduce their contribution.
- Over days, gradually continue to extend the distance, and, at the same time, ask your training partner to

reduce the amount of assistance being provided. You must decide the amount of praise and reward to give to your dog. Start by being over-generous, and reduce as you and your dog become more proficient.

- Finally, signal your training partner to slip the lead so that you can deliver the command and the dog will drop without any measurable assistance.

You are now ready to progress to the next stage, so give your dog a quality reward and thank your training partner for their invaluable help.

All dogs, regardless of age and their owner's aspirations, should be taught to drop instantaneously on command. Trouble has been avoided and many a dog's life has been saved by the timely use of this procedure.

SEND TO AND DROP

STAGE 1

The first training aid is a mat (initially about 2 ft square, then, as the dog becomes more confident, this can be reduced gradually to a 6-inch square). This piece of carpet/mat will probably be in use throughout my dog's career in Competitive Obedience. To begin with, it is used on its own as the target area for the dog to drop on to; as the exercise develops, the mat will become a confidence booster to introduce the dog to other targets.

- With the lead attached, sit the dog in the Heel position. Command the dog to "*Wait*" and "*Look*" while you place the carpet six or seven paces in front of you.

- Return to the working side of your dog and hold the lead. Again, command the dog to *"Look"*, and encourage him to gaze with a fixed stare towards the training mat.
- With a further command *"Away..."*, both dog and handler run out towards the mat. As soon as you arrive, command the dog to go *"Down"* on the mat, as you have taught in the earlier stages. Count to three, and give the dog lots and lots of praise.

The dog is being commanded to drop on the mat in a practice Send Away.

- Repeat several times until the dog is keen to dash out on his own and lie down on the mat.
- Move the mat out another two or three paces, and keep repeating this stage of training.
- Set the dog up, with the dog looking at the mat, and give the command *"Look"*.
- The dog should be keen to beat you to the mat after the command *"Away"*.
- The dog should instantly drop on the mat following the command *"Down"*.

Whatever you are teaching your dog, the most difficult aspect is to convey the exact job specification so that the dog knows exactly what to do. In my opinion, this intuitive ability to break an exercise down and teach in simple stages – ABC before WXYZ – is what separates the outstanding trainer from the average.

We know the dog will do his best to please, and, in general terms, will only misbehave or appear to deliberately mess up because he has not fully understood the task at hand. If an exercise is going wrong, take a look at the clarity and consistency of your teaching before blaming the dog.

In the preliminary exercises performed in the lower classes (and in all our earlier teaching), the handler is in close contact with the dog – almost doing the thinking to avoid mistakes, and to support and give guidance.

In the more advanced classes, during exercises such as Send Away, the dog is expected to work some distance away from you, and to think independently, and so the exercises are far more challenging.

The tests are intended to be an examination of the dog's inherited natural ability, together with how much he has benefited from your teaching. They are also a test of the dog's confidence in accomplishing elements of the test, without worrying about the handler's reaction, safe in the knowledge of mutual respect for each other.

In competition, when things go wrong (and they will), try not to overreact or be exasperated, and display massive disappointment. You will only convey displeasure and frustration to your canine partner, who will, no doubt, take total responsibility, and may suffer for days without fully understanding what he has done wrong. He will then overreact to even the simplest task, in an effort to please you. Any attempt to compete with your dog after such a setback, and before a complete recovery, will be a disaster.

STAGE 2

In our teaching, we now need to acclimatise the dog so he is ready for the show ring. With this in mind, ring posts and rope will be incorporated into a coaching session. As discussed earlier, a full ring is restrictive and intimidating, so I teach with just three electric fence

1. The handler commands the dog to "Look" at a toy, which has been placed by a post.

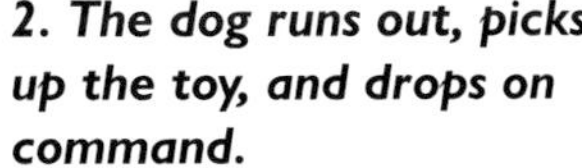

2. The dog runs out, picks up the toy, and drops on command.

posts and a length of light rope. With this equipment I can erect one side of a show ring or one corner of a show ring, both of which are ideal to practise Send Away, and to expose the dog to our next teaching aid – a post.

First, use the posts and rope to create one side of the show ring. Place the training mat (now reduced to 6 inches square) half a stride short of, and in line with, the middle post.

- Sit your dog in line with, and about 10 paces away from, the centre post.
- Instruct the dog to *"Look"*, and walk out to place the small mat in line with the centre post.
- Kneel next to the mat (on the right side), and call the dog to your right hand, which should be held out over the mat, with the fingers stretched, to make a clear target.
- When the dog arrives, encourage and, if necessary, enforce the drop on the mat. Then reward and praise the dog.
- Repeat the above steps a few times until the dog is happily completing the task to your satisfaction.
- Repeat as above, but, this time, send the dog to drop on the mat rather than calling him to you. Run out after the dog to encourage his outrun, and also to be in position to reward and praise the drop on the mat.
- Over the course of several days, repeat the exercise, slowly increasing the distance by two or three paces each time to achieve some 20 paces.

- Finally, remove the mat and line your dog up with the centre post. Command him to look straight, stand upright, and, without holding on to your dog, pause for a silent count of three. Command your dog to go "A *w a a y*.....", dropping the dog just short of the post. Now go to the dog and give loads and loads of well-deserved praise.

The next stage is to use the posts, with the ropes attached, to form or replicate one corner of a show ring:

- Sit your dog in line with, and some ten paces away from, the post.
- Instruct the dog to *"Look"* as you go out to place the mat – just short of, and in line with, the corner post.
- Repeat each step as above, remembering to give lots of praise when your dog is successful.

As stated earlier, this exercise has to be taught taking great care not to become exasperated or to show any signs of impatience. The dog must have the confidence instilled by you to achieve all the elements of the Send Away with power and enthusiasm.

As stipulated before – teach in play and make haste slowly. If the dog is struggling to understand what is expected, drop back a stage and repeat earlier teaching until the dog fully comprehends what is expected of him.

STAGE 3

We have now taught the Send Away to both a mat and a post as a precursor to the more conventional and commonly used markers. Markers can be 6-inch flower pots, plastic flags, weaving poles – in fact, just about anything to define where the judge wants the dog to drop at the end of the outrun. These markers are placed in a great variety of differing patterns, but tend to fall into two distinct categories:

1. To define the four corners of a square (of 3 or 4 feet).
2. A single marker that the dog is expected to get close to (smaller markers are sometimes used to define the boundaries of the outrun and to assist the judge in ascertaining if the outrun is in a straight line).

We should now develop our earlier teaching, taking advantage of both the mat and post schooling aids. With the electric fence posts and the light rope, erect one side of the show ring. Place four plastic flower pots (6 inches in diameter and a solid colour such as black or white) to form the corners of a three-foot (one metre) square, a stride short of the centre post. Make sure the post is in line with the centre of the box.

- Sit the dog in line with, and some ten paces away from, the box.
- Instruct the dog to *"Look"* and go out to place the mat – on the back line and centre of the box.
- Repeat each stage as above, giving lots of praise.

In the first instance, markers are used to assist and help the judge to define the drop area, and then, during the test, to define how accurate or close the dog has got to that area, thus enabling the judge to deduct marks as he/she sees fit. Typically, several marks would be lost if the dog ended up to the side of, short of, or past the marked area.

A considerate and sensible judge will ensure that markers are not used to distract or trick the dog. The judge will have considered the effect the sun will have on the test during a full day's judging, so that the morning test will be just the same as the afternoon test.

Before the Send Away area is defined, most judges will also consider the backdrop to the target vicinity to ensure it will not have a detrimental effect on their assessment.

So you can see, precision and accuracy during our teaching and subsequent training will have a tangible pay-back, as only inches (cms) will separate the top dogs on test day.

Now move the posts to replicate the corner of a show ring, and teach the rudiments of the exercise using the same methods as above.

- Remove the two flower pots and place a plastic bucket (upside down) on what was the back line of the square, and in line with the corner post. Move the two front markers forward some 3 feet (a metre) to make a triangle.

◀ ***As an additional aid a toy has been placed between markers. The dog's attention is focused on the toy, which he runs out to hold.***

▼ ***With practice, the dog will be happy to run to the Send Away box without the incentive of a toy.***

- Place the practice mat in front of the back marker (bucket).
- Teach as we have done from the early stages of Send Away, encouraging the dog to drop on to the mat from a comparatively short outrun, and then carefully increasing the distance.
- Once the dog is confidently and accurately reaching the area, remove the mat. Repeat the training, making sure the dog is confidently accomplishing the Send Away element of the exercise.

- Repeat and practise over the next few days (weeks), always starting with the small training mat. Increase the distance each day until the dog will happily go in a straight line and drop accurately and instantly some 30-40 feet away (10 or 14 metres) on the mat, to a post, to a single marker, or within a set of markers.
- Use a variety of markers and layouts to increase the dog's awareness. Always start with a small mat and a short outrun to build the dog's confidence as the distance and/or the complexity is increased.

SETTING UP A SEND AWAY

The dog, in an effort to please, may try to go to a target area that will not necessarily be the one the judge has in mind. To avoid giving the dog a choice, I have successfully used the following set-up method.

- Walk to the spot the judge wants the exercise to commence from with my dog performing very attentive Heelwork. I halt with my back directly lined up on the Send Away.
- Command the dog to come into the Present position, making sure he is perfectly straight.
- Place my right hand under the dog's chin so I can gently hold his head up while stepping to the working side of the dog.
- Use both hands as blinkers to point the dog to the Send Away.
- Command the dog to *"Look"*, and then to *"Sit"* before standing upright prior to being instructed by the judge to "send your dog".

This would obviously be perfected during several teaching and practice sessions, long before show day.

RECALL FROM THE AREA

We have already taught the dog to come to heel during Recall training, and it is natural to follow on and develop this earlier training to encompass a Recall to heel from the down position.

This is yet another example where it helps to separate the whole exercise into smaller units, and, in so doing, diminish the chances of confusing the dog. A dog anticipating the Recall out of the Send Away area is a very common fault, so the added bonus of teaching the Recall separately, and only putting the two modules together occasionally, greatly reduces the risk of this happening.

- Repeat the Recall to heel training (see page 49), starting right from the beginning, only this time when the dog is in the Down position.
- Now attach the extended lead to your dog's collar and put the dog into the Down position.
- Command the dog to *"Wait"*, and walk forward almost to the end of the extended lead. Stop, turn left, and take a couple of steps back. You are now in a position to call your dog, who will be within your range of vision.
- Call your dog using his name, followed by the command *"Heel"*. Walk forward, using the extended lead to guide the dog into position. After walking

forward together for several paces of quality Heelwork (no halts and no turns at this stage), give lots of praise.

- Continue to train in this manner until you can walk in different directions, with as many halts and turns as you wish *before* you call, but no halts or turns *after* you have called the dog.
- When you call the dog, always ensure you can see his performance, and encourage him to walk briskly to your left side. Remove the extended lead, and practise the stages as above until perfect.
- When the dog is totally confident, call him to heel when you are facing and walking towards him. Start with an extended training lead and guide the dog firmly into position, using a distinct command.
- Remove the lead, but, initially, confine the Recall to a short distance. Slowly extend the length of the Recall over a period of days, or even weeks, depending on the dog's response to your teaching.
- Sits and turns are taught in Heelwork, and there should be no need to train them during a Recall. They should only be added on an occasional basis.
- In training, only call the dog out of the Send Away area infrequently. It is far better to run up to the area to reward the dog, and leave the area with the dog doing attentive Heelwork, than to create anticipation by constantly instructing the dog to return to heel from the Send Away area.

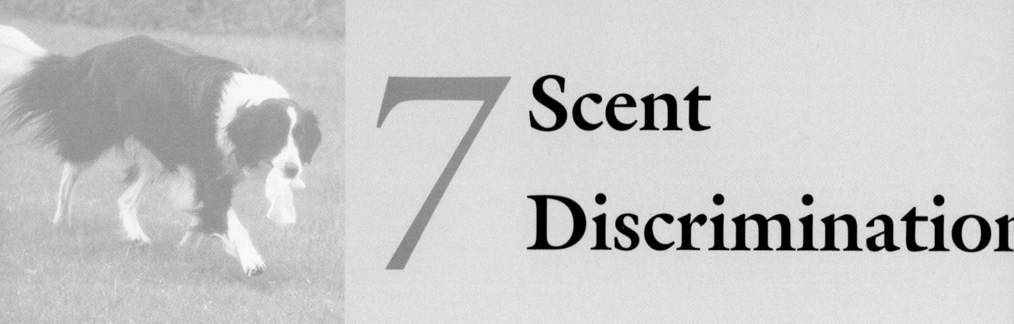

7 Scent Discrimination

Without doubt, the dog is the expert in the Scent exercise, and unless you are extremely sure, you should never question the dog's decision. Obviously, mistakes are made, but this could be because the items that are selected may be as close in smell terms as two matches made from the same sliver of wood.

If, in the show ring, your dog makes a mistake and brings in the wrong cloth, accept it and reward him with praise. Make sure you leave the ring with your head held high so as not to transmit any negative vibes to the dog.

TRAINING STRATEGY

Take care to teach this exercise with planning and forethought, slowly building to the final product. It is our job to teach the dog what is required, in a way that will not confuse or worry, and is as trouble-free as possible. Let's not kid each other: the dog is the professional. Our role is to interpret and communicate to the dog the specification and terms of the exercise.

Before teaching a formal Scent, the dog must obviously be capable of retrieve, but no other criteria is required. There is no need to wait until you have won out of the lower classes, and then attempt to teach the exercise to some self-imposed crazy timetable, because you have entered a show prior to fully teaching your dog this exercise.

There is something of the unknown and almost mystical about this test – dogs really enjoy performing it, and mostly their owners get an even bigger thrill.

Scent tests may vary depending on the regulations of your national Kennel Club, and you will need to check for specific requirements. In the United Kingdom, Scent is only performed in the three highest classes (Class 'A', 'B' and 'C'), and is always performed on cloths which are between 6 ins (15 cms) and 10 ins (25 cms).

Kennel Club rules also stipulate that the cloths will be placed at least 3 feet (1 metre), but not more than 5 feet (1.5 metre), apart.

Regulations additionally structure and formalise the total quantity of cloths, and the number of blanks and decoy cloths.

STAGE 1

One of my original training mentors recommended that I should commence my early play training with a piece of rag (about 9-10 ins/20-25 cms square, with a large knot tied in the end). The advantages of choosing this included:

- It can easily be carried in the pocket.
- It is inexpensive and easy to replace.
- It can be used for a multitude of tasks (getting and keeping the dog's attention, play retrieve and play reward to name just a few).
- It can be used as the first article for the dog to find in Scent training.

TRAINING FOR SCENT WITH IMMOVABLE OBJECTS

1. The handler gives the dog scent.

2. The dog sees the cloth being placed.

3. The dog is directed to go and search.

4. The dog searches, moving among the immovable objects.

5. The dog picks out the cloth and brings it back to his handler.

Since those early days, I have always started training with a rag, and advise all my pupils to do the same.

It is not impossible, but it is very difficult to teach this exercise on your own because of the problems of cross contamination, and resulting confusion. To teach this exercise, you need at least one training partner. You must never use, or allow, a blood relative (particularly a daughter or son) to go near a scent pattern area, nor to rub their scent on to a cloth to be used as a decoy or to scent the dog with. We all know of the outstanding, exceptional dog that never fails, but that is the exception not the rule. Throughout your dog's career, take my advice and create as near a sterile environment as possible when conducting a practice session.

SESSION ONE

- Start scent training by getting your training partner to place a row of six or seven items that your dog cannot, under any circumstances, lift or move e.g. a bucket full of sand, a house brick, a fence post.
- Sit your dog, on-lead, facing the row, and let him watch your colleague place your scent cloth out of sight, about half-way along the row.
- Give your dog scent by placing the thumb of your right hand just short of the tip of his nose, and then make a cup of your right hand over the dog's nose, without restricting the flow of air. Learn to read the signs that your dog has taken scent. My dogs will withdraw from my cupped hand to indicate that they have taken scent. When a dog is being asked to take in

other people's scent (from a cloth) it takes longer, but the withdrawal indicator is just the same.

- Stand upright, and after commanding your dog to *"Find"*, go out together to find the scent article. When the dog has picked up the cloth, walk backwards and let the dog present the article to you.
- Reward and praise your dog without going over the top and creating too much uncontrolled excitement.
- Do not immediately repeat the exercise. The dog has brought the correct item to you, and has done all that you asked of him, so you will only create confusion in the dog if you ask for an encore. Go off and do something else for an hour before repeating the exercise. Make sure your scent cloth is placed in exactly the same spot, but start scent discrimination from the other end of the row.

SESSION TWO

This is almost a repeat of the first session, but this time the dog is off the lead.

- For the first few practices, walk out with the dog to give him confidence, and verbally encourage as necessary.
- Once the dog is performing these early stages with ease, prevent him from seeing any of the articles being placed, including the correct one, by simply facing away from the row.
- Stand upright and stationary, send the dog to find the article, and, once the dog has picked up the cloth, encourage him to return to the Present position.

Try not to be uptight and tongue-tied during your Scent training. It is important to be relaxed when teaching this exercise.

In the ring, an alert judge will deduct marks for extra commands (verbal or given as body signals), but at this early stage we are training a young, inexperienced dog, who will be upset by a change in attitude.

In this early phase, don't worry about extra commands, just concentrate on keeping the dog untroubled.

Be careful not to overexcite with your actions or words, as this will deflect from your careful schooling.

SESSION THREE

Replace four (not the first or last in the row) of the immovable articles with heavy, weighted cloths.

I use envelopes of cloth that contain 1/4-inch (1/2-cm) metal plates, which sit very close to the ground. It is not impossible for the dog to move these heavyweight practice cloths, but they are not easy to pick up and are infinitely better than loose cloths.

- Continue to practise as above in Session Two. For the first couple of times, walk out towards the scenting area with the dog steady and calm, and encourage him to scent.
- As your teaching progresses, ask people (other than blood relatives) to rub a couple of cloth envelopes.

Once a dog is eagerly returning the cloth with your own

THE SCENT EXERCISE

1. Offer the dog scent from the cloth.

2. The handler sends the dog out to search.

3. The dog works his way along the line of cloths.

4. The dog picks up the cloth.

5. He brings the cloth back to his handler.

6. He comes in to the Present position, where the handler will take the cloth.

scent, introducing cloths with other people's 'hot' scent, as decoys, will not make any difference to your dog's performance. A dog will only be attracted to decoy scents if he totally lacks confidence, and such a dog is just as likely to return with a neutral or blank cloth. Often, this is because early learning has been rushed and created confusion.

It is vital to teach the rudiments of this exercise slowly and carefully. The dog is the Scent specialist; you are only channelling his natural talent to meet the requirements of the test.

It is all too easy to lose your temper and chastise your dog during Scent. However, it will take weeks of abstention from the exercise, followed by further weeks of reintroducing the exercise from the beginning, before he will have the confidence to perform in the ring. It is easy to destroy a dog's confidence – and extremely hard to restore his trust.

So far we have only practised Scent from either end of a row of articles.

Now we need to introduce other angles and scent patterns. Start by sending the dog in from a slight angle.

Then develop to sending the dog to articles/cloths placed horizontally.

All of the above scent patterns can be used in the novice classes when the dog is required to find and return with the target cloth, scented by the handler but supplied by the judge. The other five, neutral cloths are supplied by the show organisers, and all must be placed in a straight line.

Remember to make haste slowly, and at any sign of uncertainty or lack of understanding on the dog's part, drop back a stage. The dog's absolute confidence in both the exercise and in sensing your optimistic reactions, are paramount.

Now introduce other patterns: curve the cloths or articles as allowed in the more advanced classes.

Increase the number of cloths/articles. Start at 3 feet apart and increase to 5 feet.

Experiment with the pattern, but in a single training session do not change the spot your cloth occupied (you can always change the pattern by rearranging the other cloths).

When competing in the intermediate class (UK class 'B'), there must be a minimum of six cloths and a maximum of 10 (the total to include a single decoy and the target cloth scented by the handler).

In the advanced class (UK class 'C'), the minimum and maximum number of cloths used remains the same, but the target cloth is scented by the judge and decoys can be numerous. In both classes, is it up to the judge to choose the pattern.

Regulations may vary as each national Kennel Club has slightly different rules. However, the general principle of the test remains the same.

DEGREE OF DIFFICULTY

Bearing in mind that you are not allowed to give any commands, help, or encouragement to your dog, some

Scent patterns have proved to be harder than others. One of the most difficult is a large circle of neutral and decoy Scent cloths, with the cloth the dog needs to find placed on its own in the middle of the circle.

If a dog finds the correct cloth during the initial outrun, then there is normally a very good chance of a successful outcome. However, once a dog gets on to the circle, he seems to constantly scent the circle of cloths, getting more and more frantic in the process, without any attempt to scent the target cloth.

If a dog is going to challenge for a top place in the final line-up, I would practise this pattern immediately before attempting the exercise in the ring. If, however, during this element of the test, a dog displays a loss of confidence, I would give the dog all the help he needs, and then withdraw from the test. If the dog is not in a potential award position, I would advise withdrawing from competition without attempting Scent.

It is not worth messing your dog about. It is far more important to keep him happy and confident so he will perform well in all parts of the test at next week's show.

8 Distance Control

As with many of the more advanced exercises, start off training in a light-hearted, play-training style, trying not to generate tension and putting fright into your dog. Remember, a dog's hearing is many times greater than ours, so bellowing and shouting is totally unnecessary. As the handler in the ring, your task is to concentrate on delivering well-considered, clear and concise commands. These instructions will only be corrupted and distorted by shouting.

COMMANDS

Before you start teaching Distance Control (DC), you need to be aware that in the ring you are only permitted to use the dog's name followed by a single command, word or a signal for each of the six positions. It is best to fix in your mind the commands you intend to use. It could well be that, in the fullness of time, after studying your dog's response(s), you might change one or two of the commands or adjust the delivery of them, but consistency and repetition are key and great confidence-builders in early instruction.

- **SIT:** This is the most straightforward command, as long as you emphasise the 'S' and the 'T'. You will also have to decide whether to use the dog's name.

Remember, your dog is only allowed one name: if you use "Ben" for the first position, it cannot become "Bennie" for the second position. An alert judge will deduct marks for such use of the dog's name, considering it as an additional command.

- **STAND:** If we are to use a verbal command of *"Stand"* for this position, it is best not to use the 'ST' at the beginning of the word, as a keen dog will have sat long before you have delivered the rest of the word of command. For this position, use the word of command *"And"* – it gets rid of the sitting 'S' and is just as effective. My own preference for this position is the dog's name and a hand signal, but I will use the word of command (*"And"*) in all early training to underpin the hand indication of the position.

- **DOWN:** The third position command *"Down"* is normally straightforward enough, and only gets complicated if the dog insists on lying on his side (perfect positioning for a Down Stay). Many alternative commands exist: *"Flat"*, *"Drop"* and *"Lie"* are some of the suggestions, and have been used with great success by many of the top partnerships.

I teach Distance Control at various stages, starting with a young dog in his home environment. I use a play session, with me kneeling on the floor to the right, and facing the side of the dog. At this stage, the principle is to get a young dog used to the precise movements and

In recent years, it has become popular to give commands using leg signals, which work for some people and dogs. I must confess to a particular hatred of them. They look silly and ungainly, and I am not convinced they are necessary. The worst aspect is that to some people – however unjustly – they evoke cruel training methods.

the associated command. It is best to only practise two positions at a time.

STAGE ONE

FIRST COMBINATION

- The first movement taught is from the Sit to the Stand. Start with the dog positioned in the Sit.
- Hold the dog's collar in your right hand (to ensure no forward movement). Use your left hand under the puppy's belly and stretch the back legs to place him into the Stand. Give the command *"St(AND)"*, and give lots of reassurance.
- Make sure the position is held for a period of about 10 seconds.
- After this, pause, then move on to the next position to be taught: Stand to Sit.
- With your right hand still holding the collar, gently move the dog backwards. At the same time, use your left hand to sit the dog. Give the command *"SiT"* at the same time.
- Hold the position, and again quietly reward and reassure the dog for several seconds.

SECOND COMBINATION

- The third movement taught is from the Stand to the Down. Start with the dog positioned in the Stand.
- Hold the dog's collar in your right hand, and guide the dog to move backwards and to lie flat on the ground. Use your left hand to stop the dog rolling on to his side and to assist in putting the dog in position. Simultaneously, give your chosen command.
- As with previously taught movements, give reassurance, and ensure the dog holds the position for a period of about 10 seconds.
- After the pause, move on to the next position to be taught: Down to the Sit.
- Now with your left hand holding the collar, give the dog the command to "SiT", and simultaneously place the palm of your right hand on the dog's chest to assist in lifting/placing him into the Sit.
- Once more, hold the position and quietly offer reward and reassurance to the dog for several seconds before breaking off.

THIRD COMBINATION

- The fifth movement taught is from the Down to the Stand. Start with the dog positioned in the Down.
- Place the palm of your opened right hand on the dog's chest, and your left hand under the dog's belly. Command and encourage the dog to *"St(AND)"*. Make sure you use the right hand to prevent the dog moving forward.
- As before, reassure the dog and hold the position for a

period of about 10 seconds.
- Do not teach the final combination (Sit to the Down) position at this stage of training.

This early, close training should continue for as long as necessary, but you will find the dog will require less and less assistance. He will become quicker at adopting the positions, and will need increasingly less help from you. However, you will need to maintain a hands-on approach to ensure the dog makes no forward movement.

STAGE TWO

When you have arrived at the point of instant response to verbal commands, it is time to move to the next stage of training when you stand by the dog. Use an overall command to ensure the dog will know the difference between Stays and Distance Control – mine is simply "*Control*".

Remember, training is still the key word and the dog needs to be reassured and his confidence boosted at all times. Teach in short sessions, and only practise, at most, two positions at a time. Initially, it is best to teach indoors, and to remove your footwear or to wear trainers/gym shoes.

FIRST COMBINATION

- The first movement taught is from the Sit to the Stand. Start with the dog positioned in the Sit.
- Stand at the side of your dog, with your right foot across his front legs, and transferring most of your

DISTANCE CONTROL

1. Starting in the Down.

2. Signal command to Stand.

3. Verbal command to Down.

4. Signal command to Stand.

DISTANCE CONTROL

5. Signal to Sit.

6. Dog in the Sit.

7. Verbal command to Down.

8. Finally, back into the Stand.

weight to this right leg.

- Hold the lead in your left hand to stop the dog making any forward movement. Give the dog the *"AND"* command, and gently, with the left foot, assist the dog to stand. An outstretched right hand can be used to double up on the verbal command.
- Give calm reassurance and hold the position for a period of about 10 seconds.

In the early stages, break off at this point and reward your dog. Care should be taken to not overexcite the dog and undo all your hard work.

- After this break, move on to the next position to be taught: Stand to Sit. Maintain your position as described above, but transfer your weight to your left foot.
- With your left hand still holding the lead, give the command *"SiT"*, and use the lead and your right leg to gently sit the dog.
- Hold the position, and quietly reward and reassure the dog for a few seconds.

SECOND COMBINATION

- The third movement taught is from the Stand to the Down. Start with the dog positioned in the Stand.
- As for the previous group of exercises, stand with your right foot across the dog's front feet, and your left foot to the side and pointing to the rear of the dog.
- Give the command for the dog to go into the Down

position, making sure he is lying on his belly, not on his side. Using the lead, combined with your right knee and shin, encourage backward movement.

- As with the previously taught movements, make sure to convey massive reassurance.
- Hold the position for a period of about 10 seconds.

In the initial stages, break off at this point and deliver calm praise. As before, try and balance the reward – over-praise and you will add too much excitement and lose some of your control, under-praise and you risk taking the sparkle and fun away.

- After the prescribed pause, move on to the next position to be taught: Down to the Sit. Adopt the same standing position used for close control described above.
- With the lead held in your left hand, and positioned to prevent forward movement, give the dog the command to *"SiT"*.
- Simultaneously, use the lead and your right foot to encourage the dog to respond quickly.
- Hold the position, and quietly offer reward and reassurance to the dog for several seconds before breaking off.

THIRD COMBINATION

- The fifth movement taught is from the Down to the Stand. Once more, you should adopt the standing position.

- Place your right foot in front of, and across, the dog's feet. Hold the lead in your left hand to stop forward movement.
- Give the *"AND"* command, and, at the same time, transfer your weight to your right foot. Use your left foot to assist and encourage the dog into the Stand.
- As before, hold the position for some 10 seconds.

Once the dog has got used to performing this module of the exercise, you can follow up with the next position of your choice.

FINAL COMBINATION

- The last movement taught is Down from the Sit. Command the dog to drop, and prevent any forward movement or the dog rolling on to his side.
- This is a simple movement for the dog to perform, and all you need to do is to calmly encourage and reassure him.
- Once the dog has accepted and is used to performing this position, follow up with any position of your choice.

STAGE THREE

Once the dog is responding willingly and instantly to your commands, it is time to move on to the next stage and begin to add distance. I have found that, if you only move two or three paces away from your dog, the temptation is irresistible, and the dog starts to creep forward.

If you are not getting the speed and accuracy of response that you require, go back to your earlier training – but don't dwell on it. A little time spent building up mutual confidence will guarantee speed and pride in performance.

As we found before, this close training will require less and less assistance, and the dog will gradually get quicker at adopting the positions with very little assistance from you, as his confidence builds.

To ensure a performance of quality, and to keep the dog happy, you will need to regularly train Distance Control throughout his career; maintaining close contact to ensure an accurate and timely response.

- Stand your dog, and give the command *"Control"*, and walk some 12 paces away from your dog.
- Turn and face, without eyeballing your dog, and give the command for the dog to lie down on his belly. The command needs to be delivered with very little increase in volume.
- Once the dog has adopted the position, return to the working side of your dog (all exercises start and finish with the dog at your left side), after a count of three praise him for a job well done, and finish the exercise.
- To give you both confidence, practise this module of Distance Control about twice a day for a week. In parallel, we can continue the other positions on the lead as outlined in Stage Two.

- Continue to teach as above, one movement at a time, substituting Down with Sit, and so on.
- When you are ready, teach two modules together e.g. 1. Stand to Down, 2. Down to Sit, before returning to the side of your dog to give him a reward of quality.
- A week or two later, add a third position and then a fourth, building to all six.

It is good practice to move between each position, and to quietly reassure your dog between movements. Once the dog has got the message and is confident, do not always stop at six positions. In training sessions, you can do seven, eight, or only half the positions, but always be fully prepared to return to basics.

9 Obedience Shows

Before taking your dog to a show for the first time, you need to have given considerable thought to your own and your dog's needs.

As an experienced exhibitor, I would never consider taking a dog to a show for the first time to compete – the aim would be to socialise him, and to get him used to the atmosphere.

If you are new to showing, you will also need to attend several shows, just to get used to the routine, without the hassle of competing. If you are lucky enough to have someone to take you under their wing, so much the better.

IS MY DOG READY?

You must consider if your dog is ready to go to a show.

- Has he been inoculated and cleared by your veterinary surgeon as ready to go out and about?
- Have you registered your dog with the Kennel Club?
- Is your dog old enough to attend the show?
- Has your dog been socialised with people and other dogs?

If the answer to any of these questions is *No,* then you are doing more harm than good by taking your pride and joy to a show.

Initially, it is best to attend a show as a spectator, so you and your dog can become accustomed to the atmosphere.

- Sort out the veterinary situation. If you are content with treatment from a vet who prescribes homoeopathic protection, rather than conventional chemical inoculations, so be it, that's your business.
- Fill the forms in, and send them off to your national Kennel Club.
- If your dog is too young to be at the show, then don't take him. You could spend your time far more productively in your local community, socialising your dog in a far more acceptable environment of your choice.
- Do not spend your time training your dog exclusively for Competitive Obedience. It is just as important to devote your time and energy to making your dog a totally acceptable and dependable good citizen. A so-called top Obedience dog has no credence if he is a canine hooligan.

PREPARATIONS

Long before the event, most experienced exhibitors will compile a checklist of all the equipment and consumables they will need.

For the dog:

- Dog food and bowl – take your dog's regular food (this is not the time to start a new diet). It is accepted practice to feed a little less than normal before a journey and then to top up at the show.
- Drinking water – take enough for the whole day.
- Pooper scoopers, plastic bags and tissues.
- Grooming kit – a dog should look cared for, so take enough equipment to make him look good. Brush and comb your dog before working him up ready to enter the ring.
- Consideration should be given to a canine first-aid kit (often advertised for sale in the dog press).

Your requirements:

- Plenty to drink and eat – the food at shows can be very expensive and not to your liking.
- Weather forecasts can be wrong, so always be prepared for anything from freezing cold to blazing heat.
- A comprehensive first-aid kit.
- Soap and towel.
- A comfortable chair to sit on.

Most of these items can be stored in boxes and either permanently kept in your vehicle or put on board on the morning of the show.

ON THE DAY

Most Obedience shows have a great carnival atmosphere, and the car parking area becomes the venue for a social occasion with exhibitors, friends and/or relatives sitting out (weather permitting) enjoying each others' company, good food, and drink.

Once you have organised your pitch, take your dog to the designated area so he can relieve himself (making sure you clean up after him). Return to your car and offer him a drink. It is wise to let your dog have a short rest, and soak up the ambience of the show.

AT THE SHOW

Find out the booking procedure at the show. Each show you attend will vary slightly, but you will usually have to:

- Collect your ring (competitor's card) number. You will have one number per dog even though you might have entered more than one class with the same dog.
- Collect your catalogue (remember to order one on the entry form) and find out the details of the class(es) you have entered.
- Report to your class, and also find out, in each class you have entered, the time of the group Stay exercises. Write that information on the back of the ring number card for easy reference. If you do not take part in Stays you are automatically withdrawn from that class and will not be judged. It is your responsibility to be in attendance at the appropriate time and you will receive only scant sympathy if you miss out.

Now you're ready to compete – **Good luck!**